Sobriety Journal

This Journal Belongs To:

_____

"The biggest wall you gotta climb is the one you build in your mind

Do you feel bad? Do you feel like you are losing hope? Do you feel like you can't resist the urge?

IT'S OKAY!

Don't be hard on yourself! You Are AMAZING for making it this far

Better days are coming

Today's Affirmations

_____
_____
_____
_____
_____
_____
_____
_____

Today's Thoughts

_____
_____
_____
_____
_____
_____
_____
_____

How do I feel?

(1) (2) (3) (4) (5) (6) (7) (8) (9) (10)

Did I stay sober?

◯ yes   ◯ no

Date: M T W TH F SA SU

Today's Affirmations

_____
_____
_____
_____
_____
_____
_____
_____

Today's Thoughts

_____
_____
_____
_____
_____
_____
_____
_____

How do I feel?

(1) (2) (3) (4) (5) (6) (7) (8) (9) (10)

Did I stay sober?

( ) yes   ( ) no

Today's Affirmations

_____
_____
_____
_____
_____
_____
_____
_____

Today's Thoughts

_____
_____
_____
_____
_____
_____
_____

How do I feel?

(1) (2) (3) (4) (5) (6) (7) (8) (9) (10)

Did I stay sober?

( ) yes   ( ) no

Date: M   T   W   TH   F   SA   SU

Today's Affirmations

_____

_____

_____

_____

_____

_____

_____

_____

Today's Thoughts

_____

_____

_____

_____

_____

_____

_____

_____

How do I feel?

① ② ③ ④ ⑤ ⑥ ⑦ ⑧ ⑨ ⑩

Did I stay sober?

◯ yes   ◯ no

Date: _____   M T W TH F SA SU

Today's Affirmations

_____
_____
_____
_____
_____
_____
_____

Today's Thoughts

_____
_____
_____
_____
_____
_____
_____

How do I feel?

① ② ③ ④ ⑤ ⑥ ⑦ ⑧ ⑨ ⑩

Did I stay sober?

◯ yes   ◯ no

Today's Affirmations

_____

_____

_____

_____

_____

_____

_____

Today's Thoughts

_____

_____

_____

_____

_____

_____

_____

How do I feel?

① ② ③ ④ ⑤ ⑥ ⑦ ⑧ ⑨ ⑩

Did I stay sober?

◯ yes   ◯ no

Date: M   T   W   TH   F   SA   SU

Today's Affirmations

_____
_____
_____
_____
_____
_____
_____

Today's Thoughts

_____
_____
_____
_____
_____
_____
_____

How do I feel?

(1) (2) (3) (4) (5) (6) (7) (8) (9) (10)

Did I stay sober?

( ) yes   ( ) no

Date: M T W TH F SA SU

Today's Affirmations

_____
_____
_____
_____
_____
_____
_____

Today's Thoughts

_____
_____
_____
_____
_____
_____
_____

How do I feel?

① ② ③ ④ ⑤ ⑥ ⑦ ⑧ ⑨ ⑩

Did I stay sober?

◯ yes   ◯ no

Date: M   T   W   TH   F   SA   SU

Today's Affirmations

_____
_____
_____
_____
_____
_____
_____
_____

Today's Thoughts

_____
_____
_____
_____
_____
_____
_____

How do I feel?

① ② ③ ④ ⑤ ⑥ ⑦ ⑧ ⑨ ⑩

Did I stay sober?

◯ *yes*   ◯ *no*

Today's Affirmations

_____
_____
_____
_____
_____
_____
_____
_____

Today's Thoughts

_____
_____
_____
_____
_____
_____
_____

How do I feel?

① ② ③ ④ ⑤ ⑥ ⑦ ⑧ ⑨ ⑩

Did I stay sober?

◯ yes   ◯ no

Date: _____   M   T   W   TH   F   SA   SU

Today's Affirmations

_____

_____

_____

_____

_____

_____

_____

_____

Today's Thoughts

_____

_____

_____

_____

_____

_____

_____

_____

How do I feel?

① ② ③ ④ ⑤ ⑥ ⑦ ⑧ ⑨ ⑩

Did I stay sober?

◯ yes   ◯ no

Date: _____ M T W TH F SA SU

Today's Affirmations

_____
_____
_____
_____
_____
_____
_____
_____

Today's Thoughts

_____
_____
_____
_____
_____
_____
_____
_____

How do I feel?

① ② ③ ④ ⑤ ⑥ ⑦ ⑧ ⑨ ⑩

Did I stay sober?

◯ yes   ◯ no

Today's Affirmations

_____
_____
_____
_____
_____
_____
_____
_____

Today's Thoughts

_____
_____
_____
_____
_____
_____
_____

How do I feel?

① ② ③ ④ ⑤ ⑥ ⑦ ⑧ ⑨ ⑩

Did I stay sober?

◯ yes   ◯ no

Today's Affirmations

_____
_____
_____
_____
_____
_____
_____
_____

Today's Thoughts

_____
_____
_____
_____
_____
_____
_____
_____

How do I feel?

(1) (2) (3) (4) (5) (6) (7) (8) (9) (10)

Did I stay sober?

( ) yes   ( ) no

Today's Affirmations

_____
_____
_____
_____
_____
_____
_____
_____

Today's Thoughts

_____
_____
_____
_____
_____
_____
_____

How do I feel?

(1) (2) (3) (4) (5) (6) (7) (8) (9) (10)

Did I stay sober?

( ) yes   ( ) no

Today's Affirmations

_____
_____
_____
_____
_____
_____
_____
_____

Today's Thoughts

_____
_____
_____
_____
_____
_____
_____
_____

How do I feel?

(1) (2) (3) (4) (5) (6) (7) (8) (9) (10)

Did I stay sober?

( ) *yes*   ( ) *no*

Today's Affirmations

_____

_____

_____

_____

_____

_____

_____

_____

Today's Thoughts

_____

_____

_____

_____

_____

_____

_____

How do I feel?

(1) (2) (3) (4) (5) (6) (7) (8) (9) (10)

Did I stay sober?

◯ yes   ◯ no

Today's Affirmations

_____
_____
_____
_____
_____
_____
_____
_____

Today's Thoughts

_____
_____
_____
_____
_____
_____
_____
_____

How do I feel?

① ② ③ ④ ⑤ ⑥ ⑦ ⑧ ⑨ ⑩

Did I stay sober?

◯ yes   ◯ no

Today's Affirmations

_____
_____
_____
_____
_____
_____
_____
_____

Today's Thoughts

_____
_____
_____
_____
_____
_____
_____

How do I feel?

① ② ③ ④ ⑤ ⑥ ⑦ ⑧ ⑨ ⑩

Did I stay sober?

◯ yes   ◯ no

Today's Affirmations

_____
_____
_____
_____
_____
_____
_____
_____

Today's Thoughts

_____
_____
_____
_____
_____
_____
_____

How do I feel?

(1) (2) (3) (4) (5) (6) (7) (8) (9) (10)

Did I stay sober?

( ) yes   ( ) no

Date: M T W TH F SA SU

Today's Affirmations

_____
_____
_____
_____
_____
_____
_____

Today's Thoughts

_____
_____
_____
_____
_____
_____
_____

How do I feel?

① ② ③ ④ ⑤ ⑥ ⑦ ⑧ ⑨ ⑩

Did I stay sober?

◯ yes   ◯ no

Today's Affirmations

_____
_____
_____
_____
_____
_____
_____
_____
_____

Today's Thoughts

_____
_____
_____
_____
_____
_____
_____
_____

How do I feel?

① ② ③ ④ ⑤ ⑥ ⑦ ⑧ ⑨ ⑩

Did I stay sober?

◯ yes   ◯ no

M   T   W   TH   F   SA   SU

Today's Affirmations

_____
_____
_____
_____
_____
_____
_____
_____

Today's Thoughts

_____
_____
_____
_____
_____
_____
_____

How do I feel?

① ② ③ ④ ⑤ ⑥ ⑦ ⑧ ⑨ ⑩

Did I stay sober?

◯ yes   ◯ no

Today's Affirmations

_____
_____
_____
_____
_____
_____
_____
_____

Today's Thoughts

_____
_____
_____
_____
_____
_____
_____
_____
_____

How do I feel?

(1) (2) (3) (4) (5) (6) (7) (8) (9) (10)

Did I stay sober?

( ) yes   ( ) no

Today's Affirmations

_____
_____
_____
_____
_____
_____
_____
_____

Today's Thoughts

_____
_____
_____
_____
_____
_____
_____
_____

How do I feel?

① ② ③ ④ ⑤ ⑥ ⑦ ⑧ ⑨ ⑩

Did I stay sober?

◯ yes   ◯ no

Today's Affirmations

_____
_____
_____
_____
_____
_____
_____
_____

Today's Thoughts

_____
_____
_____
_____
_____
_____
_____

How do I feel?

① ② ③ ④ ⑤ ⑥ ⑦ ⑧ ⑨ ⑩

Did I stay sober?

◯ yes   ◯ no

Today's Affirmations

_____
_____
_____
_____
_____
_____
_____
_____

Today's Thoughts

_____
_____
_____
_____
_____
_____
_____
_____

How do I feel?

(1) (2) (3) (4) (5) (6) (7) (8) (9) (10)

Did I stay sober?

( ) yes   ( ) no

Date: M   T   W   TH   F   SA   SU

Today's Affirmations

_____

_____

_____

_____

_____

_____

_____

_____

Today's Thoughts

_____

_____

_____

_____

_____

_____

_____

How do I feel?

① ② ③ ④ ⑤ ⑥ ⑦ ⑧ ⑨ ⑩

Did I stay sober?

◯ yes   ◯ no

Today's Affirmations

_____

_____

_____

_____

_____

_____

_____

Today's Thoughts

_____

_____

_____

_____

_____

_____

_____

How do I feel?

① ② ③ ④ ⑤ ⑥ ⑦ ⑧ ⑨ ⑩

Did I stay sober?

◯ *yes*   ◯ *no*

Date: _____ M T W TH F SA SU

Today's Affirmations

_____
_____
_____
_____
_____
_____
_____
_____

Today's Thoughts

_____
_____
_____
_____
_____
_____
_____

How do I feel?

① ② ③ ④ ⑤ ⑥ ⑦ ⑧ ⑨ ⑩

Did I stay sober?

◯ yes   ◯ no

Today's Affirmations

_____
_____
_____
_____
_____
_____
_____
_____
_____

Today's Thoughts

_____
_____
_____
_____
_____
_____
_____
_____

How do I feel?

① ② ③ ④ ⑤ ⑥ ⑦ ⑧ ⑨ ⑩

Did I stay sober?

◯ yes   ◯ no

Today's Affirmations

_____
_____
_____
_____
_____
_____
_____

Today's Thoughts

_____
_____
_____
_____
_____
_____

How do I feel?

① ② ③ ④ ⑤ ⑥ ⑦ ⑧ ⑨ ⑩

Did I stay sober?

◯ yes   ◯ no

Today's Affirmations

_____
_____
_____
_____
_____
_____
_____
_____

Today's Thoughts

_____
_____
_____
_____
_____
_____
_____

How do I feel?

(1) (2) (3) (4) (5) (6) (7) (8) (9) (10)

Did I stay sober?

◯ yes   ◯ no

Today's Affirmations

_____
_____
_____
_____
_____
_____
_____
_____

Today's Thoughts

_____
_____
_____
_____
_____
_____
_____

How do I feel?

(1) (2) (3) (4) (5) (6) (7) (8) (9) (10)

Did I stay sober?

( ) yes   ( ) no

Today's Affirmations

_____
_____
_____
_____
_____
_____
_____
_____

Today's Thoughts

_____
_____
_____
_____
_____
_____
_____

How do I feel?

(1) (2) (3) (4) (5) (6) (7) (8) (9) (10)

Did I stay sober?

◯ yes   ◯ no

Today's Affirmations

_____
_____
_____
_____
_____
_____
_____
_____

Today's Thoughts

_____
_____
_____
_____
_____
_____
_____
_____

How do I feel?

① ② ③ ④ ⑤ ⑥ ⑦ ⑧ ⑨ ⑩

Did I stay sober?

◯ yes   ◯ no

Today's Affirmations

_____
_____
_____
_____
_____
_____
_____
_____

Today's Thoughts

_____
_____
_____
_____
_____
_____
_____

How do I feel?

(1) (2) (3) (4) (5) (6) (7) (8) (9) (10)

Did I stay sober?

( ) yes   ( ) no

Today's Affirmations

_____
_____
_____
_____
_____
_____
_____
_____
_____

Today's Thoughts

_____
_____
_____
_____
_____
_____
_____
_____
_____

How do I feel?

① ② ③ ④ ⑤ ⑥ ⑦ ⑧ ⑨ ⑩

Did I stay sober?

◯ yes   ◯ no

Date: M   T   W   TH   F   SA   SU

Today's Affirmations

_____
_____
_____
_____
_____
_____
_____
_____

Today's Thoughts

_____
_____
_____
_____
_____
_____
_____

How do I feel?

① ② ③ ④ ⑤ ⑥ ⑦ ⑧ ⑨ ⑩

Did I stay sober?

◯ yes   ◯ no

Today's Affirmations

_____
_____
_____
_____
_____
_____
_____
_____

Today's Thoughts

_____
_____
_____
_____
_____
_____
_____

How do I feel?

(1) (2) (3) (4) (5) (6) (7) (8) (9) (10)

Did I stay sober?

◯ yes   ◯ no

Date: _____　　　M　T　W　TH　F　SA　SU

Today's Affirmations

_____
_____
_____
_____
_____
_____
_____
_____

Today's Thoughts

_____
_____
_____
_____
_____
_____
_____
_____

How do I feel?

① ② ③ ④ ⑤ ⑥ ⑦ ⑧ ⑨ ⑩

Did I stay sober?

◯ yes　　　◯ no

Today's Affirmations

_____
_____
_____
_____
_____
_____
_____
_____

Today's Thoughts

_____
_____
_____
_____
_____
_____
_____
_____

How do I feel?

① ② ③ ④ ⑤ ⑥ ⑦ ⑧ ⑨ ⑩

Did I stay sober?

◯ yes   ◯ no

Today's Affirmations

_____

_____

_____

_____

_____

_____

_____

_____

Today's Thoughts

_____

_____

_____

_____

_____

_____

_____

How do I feel?

① ② ③ ④ ⑤ ⑥ ⑦ ⑧ ⑨ ⑩

Did I stay sober?

◯ yes   ◯ no

Today's Affirmations

_____
_____
_____
_____
_____
_____
_____
_____

Today's Thoughts

_____
_____
_____
_____
_____
_____
_____
_____

How do I feel?

(1) (2) (3) (4) (5) (6) (7) (8) (9) (10)

Did I stay sober?

◯ yes   ◯ no

Today's Affirmations

_____
_____
_____
_____
_____
_____
_____
_____

Today's Thoughts

_____
_____
_____
_____
_____
_____
_____
_____

How do I feel?

(1) (2) (3) (4) (5) (6) (7) (8) (9) (10)

Did I stay sober?

◯ yes   ◯ no

Today's Affirmations

_____
_____
_____
_____
_____
_____
_____
_____

Today's Thoughts

_____
_____
_____
_____
_____
_____
_____
_____

How do I feel?

① ② ③ ④ ⑤ ⑥ ⑦ ⑧ ⑨ ⑩

Did I stay sober?

◯ *yes*   ◯ *no*

Today's Affirmations

_____
_____
_____
_____
_____
_____
_____
_____

Today's Thoughts

_____
_____
_____
_____
_____
_____
_____

How do I feel?

① ② ③ ④ ⑤ ⑥ ⑦ ⑧ ⑨ ⑩

Did I stay sober?

◯ yes   ◯ no

Today's Affirmations

_____
_____
_____
_____
_____
_____
_____
_____

Today's Thoughts

_____
_____
_____
_____
_____
_____
_____
_____

How do I feel?

(1) (2) (3) (4) (5) (6) (7) (8) (9) (10)

Did I stay sober?

◯ yes   ◯ no

Date: M   T   W   TH   F   SA   SU

Today's Affirmations

_____

_____

_____

_____

_____

_____

_____

_____

Today's Thoughts

_____

_____

_____

_____

_____

_____

_____

_____

How do I feel?

(1) (2) (3) (4) (5) (6) (7) (8) (9) (10)

Did I stay sober?

◯ *yes*   ◯ *no*

Date: M   T   W   TH   F   SA   SU

Today's Affirmations

_____

Today's Thoughts

_____

How do I feel?

(1) (2) (3) (4) (5) (6) (7) (8) (9) (10)

Did I stay sober?

( ) *yes*   ( ) *no*

Today's Affirmations

_____
_____
_____
_____
_____
_____
_____
_____

Today's Thoughts

_____
_____
_____
_____
_____
_____
_____

How do I feel?

(1) (2) (3) (4) (5) (6) (7) (8) (9) (10)

Did I stay sober?

◯ yes   ◯ no

Date: M   T   W   TH   F   SA   SU

Today's Affirmations

_____
_____
_____
_____
_____
_____
_____
_____

Today's Thoughts

_____
_____
_____
_____
_____
_____
_____
_____

How do I feel?

(1) (2) (3) (4) (5) (6) (7) (8) (9) (10)

Did I stay sober?

◯ yes   ◯ no

Today's Affirmations

_____
_____
_____
_____
_____
_____
_____
_____

Today's Thoughts

_____
_____
_____
_____
_____
_____
_____

How do I feel?

① ② ③ ④ ⑤ ⑥ ⑦ ⑧ ⑨ ⑩

Did I stay sober?

◯ yes   ◯ no

Today's Affirmations

_____

_____

_____

_____

_____

_____

_____

Today's Thoughts

_____

_____

_____

_____

_____

_____

_____

How do I feel?

① ② ③ ④ ⑤ ⑥ ⑦ ⑧ ⑨ ⑩

Did I stay sober?

◯ yes   ◯ no

Today's Affirmations

_____
_____
_____
_____
_____
_____
_____
_____

Today's Thoughts

_____
_____
_____
_____
_____
_____
_____

How do I feel?

(1) (2) (3) (4) (5) (6) (7) (8) (9) (10)

Did I stay sober?

◯ yes   ◯ no

Date: M   T   W   TH   F   SA   SU

Today's Affirmations

_____
_____
_____
_____
_____
_____
_____
_____

Today's Thoughts

_____
_____
_____
_____
_____
_____
_____
_____

How do I feel?

(1) (2) (3) (4) (5) (6) (7) (8) (9) (10)

Did I stay sober?

( ) yes   ( ) no

Today's Affirmations

_____
_____
_____
_____
_____
_____
_____
_____

Today's Thoughts

_____
_____
_____
_____
_____
_____
_____
_____

How do I feel?

① ② ③ ④ ⑤ ⑥ ⑦ ⑧ ⑨ ⑩

Did I stay sober?

◯ yes   ◯ no

Today's Affirmations

_____

_____

_____

_____

_____

_____

_____

_____

Today's Thoughts

_____

_____

_____

_____

_____

_____

_____

_____

How do I feel?

① ② ③ ④ ⑤ ⑥ ⑦ ⑧ ⑨ ⑩

Did I stay sober?

◯ yes   ◯ no

Date: M   T   W   TH   F   SA   SU

Today's Affirmations

_____
_____
_____
_____
_____
_____
_____
_____

Today's Thoughts

_____
_____
_____
_____
_____
_____
_____

How do I feel?

① ② ③ ④ ⑤ ⑥ ⑦ ⑧ ⑨ ⑩

Did I stay sober?

◯ yes   ◯ no

Date: M   T   W   TH   F   SA   SU

Today's Affirmations

_____
_____
_____
_____
_____
_____
_____
_____

Today's Thoughts

_____
_____
_____
_____
_____
_____
_____
_____

How do I feel?

① ② ③ ④ ⑤ ⑥ ⑦ ⑧ ⑨ ⑩

Did I stay sober?

◯ yes   ◯ no

Today's Affirmations

_____
_____
_____
_____
_____
_____
_____

Today's Thoughts

_____
_____
_____
_____
_____
_____
_____

How do I feel?

① ② ③ ④ ⑤ ⑥ ⑦ ⑧ ⑨ ⑩

Did I stay sober?

◯ yes   ◯ no

Date: M   T   W   TH   F   SA   SU

Today's Affirmations

_____
_____
_____
_____
_____
_____
_____
_____

Today's Thoughts

_____
_____
_____
_____
_____
_____
_____
_____

How do I feel?

(1) (2) (3) (4) (5) (6) (7) (8) (9) (10)

Did I stay sober?

( ) yes   ( ) no

Today's Affirmations

_____
_____
_____
_____
_____
_____
_____
_____

Today's Thoughts

_____
_____
_____
_____
_____
_____
_____

How do I feel?

① ② ③ ④ ⑤ ⑥ ⑦ ⑧ ⑨ ⑩

Did I stay sober?

◯ yes   ◯ no

Date: M   T   W   TH   F   SA   SU

Today's Affirmations

_____
_____
_____
_____
_____
_____
_____
_____
_____

Today's Thoughts

_____
_____
_____
_____
_____
_____
_____
_____

How do I feel?

(1) (2) (3) (4) (5) (6) (7) (8) (9) (10)

Did I stay sober?

( ) yes   ( ) no

Today's Affirmations

_____
_____
_____
_____
_____
_____
_____
_____

Today's Thoughts

_____
_____
_____
_____
_____
_____
_____

How do I feel?

① ② ③ ④ ⑤ ⑥ ⑦ ⑧ ⑨ ⑩

Did I stay sober?

◯ yes   ◯ no

Date: M   T   W   TH   F   SA   SU

Today's Affirmations

_____
_____
_____
_____
_____
_____
_____
_____

Today's Thoughts

_____
_____
_____
_____
_____
_____
_____

How do I feel?

① ② ③ ④ ⑤ ⑥ ⑦ ⑧ ⑨ ⑩

Did I stay sober?

◯ yes   ◯ no

Today's Affirmations

_____
_____
_____
_____
_____
_____
_____

Today's Thoughts

_____
_____
_____
_____
_____
_____
_____

How do I feel?

(1) (2) (3) (4) (5) (6) (7) (8) (9) (10)

Did I stay sober?

( ) yes   ( ) no

Date: M   T   W   TH   F   SA   SU

Today's Affirmations

_____
_____
_____
_____
_____
_____
_____
_____

Today's Thoughts

_____
_____
_____
_____
_____
_____
_____

How do I feel?

① ② ③ ④ ⑤ ⑥ ⑦ ⑧ ⑨ ⑩

Did I stay sober?

◯ yes   ◯ no

Today's Affirmations

_____

_____

_____

_____

_____

_____

_____

_____

Today's Thoughts

_____

_____

_____

_____

_____

_____

_____

How do I feel?

(1) (2) (3) (4) (5) (6) (7) (8) (9) (10)

Did I stay sober?

◯ *yes*   ◯ *no*

Today's Affirmations

_____
_____
_____
_____
_____
_____
_____
_____

Today's Thoughts

_____
_____
_____
_____
_____
_____
_____
_____

How do I feel?

① ② ③ ④ ⑤ ⑥ ⑦ ⑧ ⑨ ⑩

Did I stay sober?

◯ yes   ◯ no

Today's Affirmations

_____
_____
_____
_____
_____
_____
_____
_____

Today's Thoughts

_____
_____
_____
_____
_____
_____
_____

How do I feel?

(1) (2) (3) (4) (5) (6) (7) (8) (9) (10)

Did I stay sober?

( ) yes   ( ) no

Today's Affirmations

_____
_____
_____
_____
_____
_____
_____
_____

Today's Thoughts

_____
_____
_____
_____
_____
_____
_____
_____

How do I feel?

(1) (2) (3) (4) (5) (6) (7) (8) (9) (10)

Did I stay sober?

( ) yes   ( ) no

Date: M   T   W   TH   F   SA   SU

Today's Affirmations

_____
_____
_____
_____
_____
_____
_____

Today's Thoughts

_____
_____
_____
_____
_____
_____
_____

How do I feel?

① ② ③ ④ ⑤ ⑥ ⑦ ⑧ ⑨ ⑩

Did I stay sober?

◯ yes   ◯ no

Today's Affirmations

_____
_____
_____
_____
_____
_____
_____
_____

Today's Thoughts

_____
_____
_____
_____
_____
_____
_____

How do I feel?

(1) (2) (3) (4) (5) (6) (7) (8) (9) (10)

Did I stay sober?

◯ yes   ◯ no

Today's Affirmations

_____
_____
_____
_____
_____
_____
_____

Today's Thoughts

_____
_____
_____
_____
_____
_____
_____

How do I feel?

(1) (2) (3) (4) (5) (6) (7) (8) (9) (10)

Did I stay sober?

◯ yes   ◯ no

Date: M T W TH F SA SU

Today's Affirmations

_____
_____
_____
_____
_____
_____
_____
_____
_____

Today's Thoughts

_____
_____
_____
_____
_____
_____
_____
_____

How do I feel?

① ② ③ ④ ⑤ ⑥ ⑦ ⑧ ⑨ ⑩

Did I stay sober?

◯ yes   ◯ no

Today's Affirmations

_____

_____

_____

_____

_____

_____

_____

Today's Thoughts

_____

_____

_____

_____

_____

_____

_____

How do I feel?

(1) (2) (3) (4) (5) (6) (7) (8) (9) (10)

Did I stay sober?

◯ *yes*   ◯ *no*

Today's Affirmations

_____
_____
_____
_____
_____
_____
_____
_____
_____

Today's Thoughts

_____
_____
_____
_____
_____
_____
_____

How do I feel?

(1) (2) (3) (4) (5) (6) (7) (8) (9) (10)

Did I stay sober?

( ) yes   ( ) no

Today's Affirmations

_____
_____
_____
_____
_____
_____
_____
_____

Today's Thoughts

_____
_____
_____
_____
_____
_____
_____
_____

How do I feel?

① ② ③ ④ ⑤ ⑥ ⑦ ⑧ ⑨ ⑩

Did I stay sober?

◯ yes   ◯ no

Today's Affirmations

_____
_____
_____
_____
_____
_____
_____
_____

Today's Thoughts

_____
_____
_____
_____
_____
_____
_____

How do I feel?

(1) (2) (3) (4) (5) (6) (7) (8) (9) (10)

Did I stay sober?

◯ yes   ◯ no

Date: _____   M   T   W   TH   F   SA   SU

Today's Affirmations

_____
_____
_____
_____
_____
_____
_____
_____

Today's Thoughts

_____
_____
_____
_____
_____
_____
_____

How do I feel?

(1) (2) (3) (4) (5) (6) (7) (8) (9) (10)

Did I stay sober?

◯ yes   ◯ no

Today's Affirmations

_____

_____

_____

_____

_____

_____

_____

_____

Today's Thoughts

_____

_____

_____

_____

_____

_____

_____

_____

How do I feel?

① ② ③ ④ ⑤ ⑥ ⑦ ⑧ ⑨ ⑩

Did I stay sober?

◯ yes   ◯ no

Date: M   T   W   TH   F   SA   SU

Today's Affirmations

_____
_____
_____
_____
_____
_____
_____
_____

Today's Thoughts

_____
_____
_____
_____
_____
_____
_____

How do I feel?

(1) (2) (3) (4) (5) (6) (7) (8) (9) (10)

Did I stay sober?

◯ yes   ◯ no

Date: M   T   W   TH   F   SA   SU

Today's Affirmations

_____
_____
_____
_____
_____
_____
_____
_____

Today's Thoughts

_____
_____
_____
_____
_____
_____
_____
_____

How do I feel?

① ② ③ ④ ⑤ ⑥ ⑦ ⑧ ⑨ ⑩

Did I stay sober?

◯ yes   ◯ no

Date: _____   M   T   W   TH   F   SA   SU

Today's Affirmations

_____
_____
_____
_____
_____
_____
_____

Today's Thoughts

_____
_____
_____
_____
_____
_____
_____

How do I feel?

(1) (2) (3) (4) (5) (6) (7) (8) (9) (10)

Did I stay sober?

◯ yes   ◯ no

Today's Affirmations

_____
_____
_____
_____
_____
_____
_____
_____
_____

Today's Thoughts

_____
_____
_____
_____
_____
_____
_____
_____

How do I feel?

① ② ③ ④ ⑤ ⑥ ⑦ ⑧ ⑨ ⑩

Did I stay sober?

◯ yes   ◯ no

Date: M   T   W   TH   F   SA   SU

Today's Affirmations

_____
_____
_____
_____
_____
_____
_____
_____

Today's Thoughts

_____
_____
_____
_____
_____
_____
_____

How do I feel?

(1) (2) (3) (4) (5) (6) (7) (8) (9) (10)

Did I stay sober?

( ) yes   ( ) no

Date: M   T   W   TH   F   SA   SU

Today's Affirmations

Today's Thoughts

How do I feel?

① ② ③ ④ ⑤ ⑥ ⑦ ⑧ ⑨ ⑩

Did I stay sober?

◯ *yes*   ◯ *no*

Today's Affirmations

_____

_____

_____

_____

_____

_____

_____

_____

Today's Thoughts

_____

_____

_____

_____

_____

_____

_____

How do I feel?

① ② ③ ④ ⑤ ⑥ ⑦ ⑧ ⑨ ⑩

Did I stay sober?

◯ yes   ◯ no

Date: M   T   W   TH   F   SA   SU

Today's Affirmations

_____
_____
_____
_____
_____
_____
_____
_____
_____

Today's Thoughts

_____
_____
_____
_____
_____
_____
_____
_____

How do I feel?

① ② ③ ④ ⑤ ⑥ ⑦ ⑧ ⑨ ⑩

Did I stay sober?

◯ yes   ◯ no

Today's Affirmations

_____
_____
_____
_____
_____
_____
_____
_____

Today's Thoughts

_____
_____
_____
_____
_____
_____
_____

How do I feel?

① ② ③ ④ ⑤ ⑥ ⑦ ⑧ ⑨ ⑩

Did I stay sober?

◯ yes   ◯ no

Today's Affirmations

_____
_____
_____
_____
_____
_____
_____
_____
_____

Today's Thoughts

_____
_____
_____
_____
_____
_____
_____
_____
_____

How do I feel?

① ② ③ ④ ⑤ ⑥ ⑦ ⑧ ⑨ ⑩

Did I stay sober?

◯ yes   ◯ no

Date: M   T   W   TH   F   SA   SU

Today's Affirmations

_____
_____
_____
_____
_____
_____
_____

Today's Thoughts

_____
_____
_____
_____
_____
_____
_____

How do I feel?

(1) (2) (3) (4) (5) (6) (7) (8) (9) (10)

Did I stay sober?

◯ yes   ◯ no

Date: M   T   W   TH   F   SA   SU

Today's Affirmations

_____
_____
_____
_____
_____
_____
_____
_____

Today's Thoughts

_____
_____
_____
_____
_____
_____
_____

How do I feel?

(1) (2) (3) (4) (5) (6) (7) (8) (9) (10)

Did I stay sober?

◯ yes   ◯ no

Today's Affirmations

_____

_____

_____

_____

_____

_____

_____

_____

Today's Thoughts

_____

_____

_____

_____

_____

_____

_____

How do I feel?

(1) (2) (3) (4) (5) (6) (7) (8) (9) (10)

Did I stay sober?

◯ yes   ◯ no

Today's Affirmations

_____
_____
_____
_____
_____
_____
_____
_____
_____

Today's Thoughts

_____
_____
_____
_____
_____
_____
_____
_____

How do I feel?

① ② ③ ④ ⑤ ⑥ ⑦ ⑧ ⑨ ⑩

Did I stay sober?

◯ yes   ◯ no

Today's Affirmations

_____
_____
_____
_____
_____
_____
_____

Today's Thoughts

_____
_____
_____
_____
_____
_____
_____

How do I feel?

① ② ③ ④ ⑤ ⑥ ⑦ ⑧ ⑨ ⑩

Did I stay sober?

◯ yes   ◯ no

Today's Affirmations

_____
_____
_____
_____
_____
_____
_____
_____
_____

Today's Thoughts

_____
_____
_____
_____
_____
_____
_____
_____

How do I feel?

① ② ③ ④ ⑤ ⑥ ⑦ ⑧ ⑨ ⑩

Did I stay sober?

◯ yes   ◯ no

Today's Affirmations

_____
_____
_____
_____
_____
_____
_____
_____

Today's Thoughts

_____
_____
_____
_____
_____
_____
_____

How do I feel?

(1) (2) (3) (4) (5) (6) (7) (8) (9) (10)

Did I stay sober?

◯ yes   ◯ no

Date: _____   M   T   W   TH   F   SA   SU

Today's Affirmations

_____
_____
_____
_____
_____
_____
_____
_____
_____

Today's Thoughts

_____
_____
_____
_____
_____
_____
_____
_____

How do I feel?

(1) (2) (3) (4) (5) (6) (7) (8) (9) (10)

Did I stay sober?

◯ yes   ◯ no

Today's Affirmations

_____
_____
_____
_____
_____
_____
_____
_____

Today's Thoughts

_____
_____
_____
_____
_____
_____
_____

How do I feel?

① ② ③ ④ ⑤ ⑥ ⑦ ⑧ ⑨ ⑩

Did I stay sober?

◯ *yes*   ◯ *no*

Date: _____ M T W TH F SA SU

Today's Affirmations

_____
_____
_____
_____
_____
_____
_____
_____
_____

Today's Thoughts

_____
_____
_____
_____
_____
_____
_____
_____

How do I feel?

(1) (2) (3) (4) (5) (6) (7) (8) (9) (10)

Did I stay sober?

◯ yes   ◯ no

Today's Affirmations

_____
_____
_____
_____
_____
_____
_____
_____

Today's Thoughts

_____
_____
_____
_____
_____
_____
_____

How do I feel?

(1) (2) (3) (4) (5) (6) (7) (8) (9) (10)

Did I stay sober?

◯ yes   ◯ no

Date: M T W TH F SA SU

Today's Affirmations

_____
_____
_____
_____
_____
_____
_____
_____

Today's Thoughts

_____
_____
_____
_____
_____
_____
_____

How do I feel?

① ② ③ ④ ⑤ ⑥ ⑦ ⑧ ⑨ ⑩

Did I stay sober?

◯ yes   ◯ no

Date: M   T   W   TH   F   SA   SU

Today's Affirmations

_____
_____
_____
_____
_____
_____
_____
_____

Today's Thoughts

_____
_____
_____
_____
_____
_____
_____

How do I feel?

① ② ③ ④ ⑤ ⑥ ⑦ ⑧ ⑨ ⑩

Did I stay sober?

◯ yes   ◯ no

Today's Affirmations

_____
_____
_____
_____
_____
_____
_____
_____
_____

Today's Thoughts

_____
_____
_____
_____
_____
_____
_____
_____

How do I feel?

(1) (2) (3) (4) (5) (6) (7) (8) (9) (10)

Did I stay sober?

( ) yes   ( ) no

Today's Affirmations

_____
_____
_____
_____
_____
_____
_____
_____

Today's Thoughts

_____
_____
_____
_____
_____
_____
_____
_____

How do I feel?

(1) (2) (3) (4) (5) (6) (7) (8) (9) (10)

Did I stay sober?

◯ yes   ◯ no

Date: _____   M   T   W   TH   F   SA   SU

Today's Affirmations

_____
_____
_____
_____
_____
_____
_____
_____

Today's Thoughts

_____
_____
_____
_____
_____
_____
_____

How do I feel?

(1) (2) (3) (4) (5) (6) (7) (8) (9) (10)

Did I stay sober?

◯ yes   ◯ no

Today's Affirmations

_____
_____
_____
_____
_____
_____
_____
_____

Today's Thoughts

_____
_____
_____
_____
_____
_____
_____

How do I feel?

(1) (2) (3) (4) (5) (6) (7) (8) (9) (10)

Did I stay sober?

◯ yes   ◯ no

Date: M   T   W   TH   F   SA SU

Today's Affirmations

_____
_____
_____
_____
_____
_____
_____
_____

Today's Thoughts

_____
_____
_____
_____
_____
_____
_____

How do I feel?

① ② ③ ④ ⑤ ⑥ ⑦ ⑧ ⑨ ⑩

Did I stay sober?

◯ yes   ◯ no

Date: _____ M T W TH F SA SU

Today's Affirmations

_____
_____
_____
_____
_____
_____
_____
_____

Today's Thoughts

_____
_____
_____
_____
_____
_____
_____

How do I feel?

(1) (2) (3) (4) (5) (6) (7) (8) (9) (10)

Did I stay sober?

◯ yes   ◯ no

Date: M   T   W   TH   F   SA   SU

Today's Affirmations

_____
_____
_____
_____
_____
_____
_____
_____
_____

Today's Thoughts

_____
_____
_____
_____
_____
_____
_____
_____

How do I feel?

① ② ③ ④ ⑤ ⑥ ⑦ ⑧ ⑨ ⑩

Did I stay sober?

◯ yes   ◯ no

Date: M   T   W   TH   F   SA   SU

Today's Affirmations

_____
_____
_____
_____
_____
_____
_____
_____

Today's Thoughts

_____
_____
_____
_____
_____
_____
_____

How do I feel?

① ② ③ ④ ⑤ ⑥ ⑦ ⑧ ⑨ ⑩

Did I stay sober?

◯ yes   ◯ no

Date: _____   M T W TH F SA SU

Today's Affirmations

_____
_____
_____
_____
_____
_____
_____
_____
_____
_____

Today's Thoughts

_____
_____
_____
_____
_____
_____
_____
_____

How do I feel?

(1) (2) (3) (4) (5) (6) (7) (8) (9) (10)

Did I stay sober?

( ) yes   ( ) no

Today's Affirmations

_____
_____
_____
_____
_____
_____
_____
_____

Today's Thoughts

_____
_____
_____
_____
_____
_____
_____

How do I feel?

(1) (2) (3) (4) (5) (6) (7) (8) (9) (10)

Did I stay sober?

( ) yes   ( ) no

Date: M   T   W   TH   F   SA   SU

Today's Affirmations

_____
_____
_____
_____
_____
_____
_____
_____

Today's Thoughts

_____
_____
_____
_____
_____
_____
_____

How do I feel?

① ② ③ ④ ⑤ ⑥ ⑦ ⑧ ⑨ ⑩

Did I stay sober?

◯ yes   ◯ no

Today's Affirmations

_____
_____
_____
_____
_____
_____
_____
_____

Today's Thoughts

_____
_____
_____
_____
_____
_____
_____

How do I feel?

① ② ③ ④ ⑤ ⑥ ⑦ ⑧ ⑨ ⑩

Did I stay sober?

◯ yes   ◯ no

.

Made in the USA
Columbia, SC
31 March 2019